8.2022

Dear Cora,
I hope to meet
you one day! Have so
much fun with this
book! Enjoy!
Yay to Yoga *
with love,
Mari * + Ronnie ♡
the
Frog

MW01154758

YAY FOR YOGA!

By Mari Irwin | Illustrations by Dabin Han

RPSS - ROCK PAPER SAFETY SCISSORS PUBLISHING
BUFFALO, NEW YORK

RPSS - Rock, Paper, Safety Scissors Publishing,
429 Englewood Avenue, Kenmore, NY 14223
publisher@rockpapersafetyscissors.com

Library of Congress Control Number: 2021921615

ISBN-13: 978-1-956688-07-8

Yay For Yoga! - Hardcover

18 19 20 21 22 6 5 4 3 2 1

--

Published for Mari Fox Wellness

First Printing: 2022

Printed in the USA

This book is dedicated to my Love, Jamie.

Thank you for your unconditional love

and unwavering encouragement

on this beloved project.

A million thanks to my "cheerleaders" and amazing "Thought Partners" including Jamie, Jenny, and Mike. Dabin, thank you for bringing my ideas to life through your hard work and magnificent illustrations. Laura Faye, I am so grateful for your partnership and creative sparkles.

Hi! I'm Mari and this
is my friend, Ronnie.
We both love Yoga and we
want to share it with you!

Yoga is a wonderful little word
that makes Ronnie and me happy
and it can help you feel calm, too!

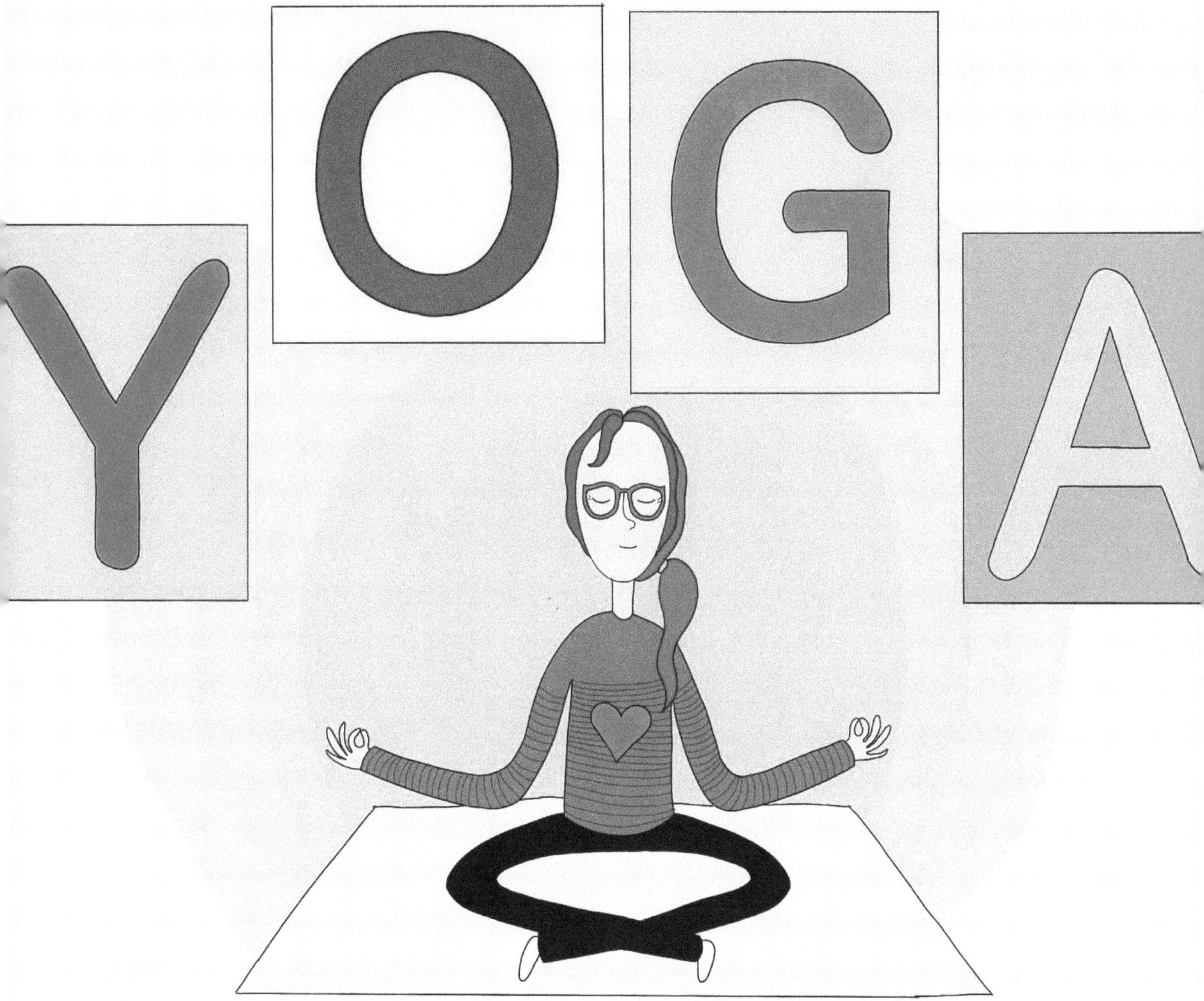
Y O G A

Yoga is about making fun shapes with your body, breathing in and out.

Yoga is about being kind to yourself and others.

Yoga is about being kind to animals, nature and other creatures.

Our minds can be so busy and noisy!

We can feel like we are swimming
in a sea of sounds, information,
colors, projects, people, and places.

Yoga can help us to get focused and relaxed.

Before practicing, it is important
to put away anything that distracts you
so we can build our focus and
concentration muscles.

Let's begin by making some
fun shapes with our body!

Arms wide to make the letter Y.

Fingers connect overhead
to make a big letter O.

Arms overhead and curved
to the side to make a big letter G.

Arms lift up over your head
with fingertips touching
to make a letter A.

What does

Y-O-G-A

spell?

It spells Yoga!

When we practice Yoga, we are not competing with anyone. We do not need a mirror. It is time to breathe and be safe with ourselves and our bodies. We can do this in a classroom, a quiet place, our bed, our school, and even a tent. Yoga can be practiced anywhere, even outside among trees, animals, and buildings!

All you need are comfy clothes and if you like, take off your shoes and socks. Your feet like to breathe and be free!

Let's start by walking slowly all over the Yoga mat or towel. Feel what is under your feet.

How does it feel?

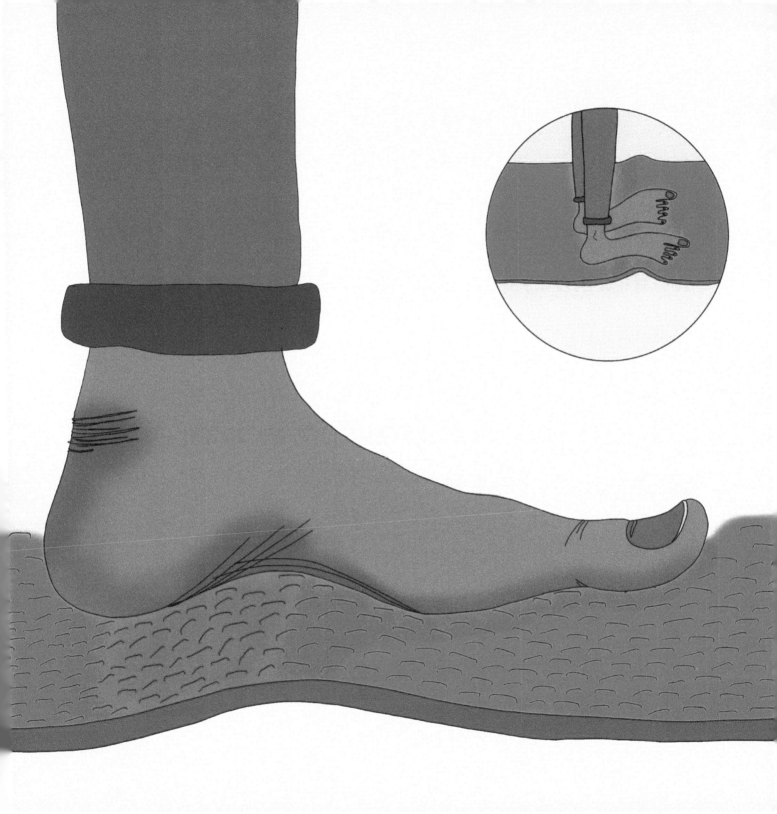

If you have a Yoga mat or a towel, unroll it and smooth it out to lie flat on the ground.

You can still do the fun poses with or without a Yoga mat!

BUG: Try lying on your back like a bug. Shake, shake, shake your arms and legs like a bug that got stuck on its back. Shake your body and then freeze! Be silly and then be still.

What do you feel in your body at this moment?

TWIST: Lie on your back, bring your knees in, and then lower your knees slowly to one side. Breathe in and out and then bring both knees to the other side. Take another breath here.

Feel the twist? It's so good for your body!

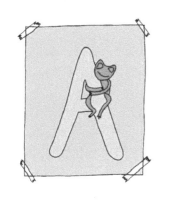

ROCK AND ROLL: Now bring in your knees to your chest and start to hug them with your arms. Rock forward and back a few times and then roll side to side to massage your amazing back muscles.

TABLE POSE: Come to your hands and knees and imagine that someone is going to set a tray of rubber duckies or cupcakes on your back. Breathe and be a strong, still table.

Do these poses feel good in your body?

UPDOG: Starting on your belly, place your hands flat on the floor under your shoulders and press yourself up with straight arms. Your legs are straight back behind you.

TABLE POSE EXTENDED: From table pose, try lifting the one leg back in line with the hip. If you are breathing smoothly and feel steady, reach the opposite arm forward with the thumb facing the ceiling. Come back to table pose and try this on the other side.

DOWNWARD DOG 🐾: Pets do Yoga, too!
Dogs naturally stretch into this pose. Have you ever seen a dog do this pose?

What is your breath doing when you try these poses?

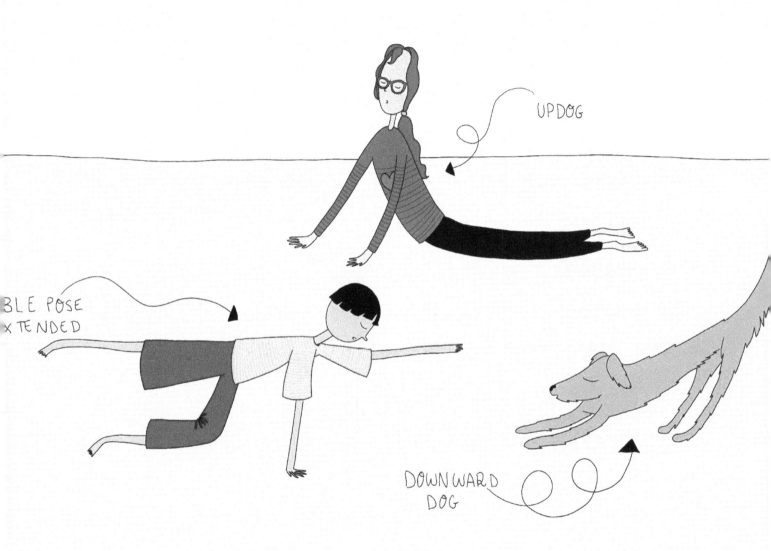

LADYBUG: With wide legs, squat down and bring your hands together in front of your heart. See if you can be still and quiet like a ladybug and breathe here for a few breaths.

DOWNWARD DOG: Start in table pose, tuck your toes under, press yourself up to an upside-down V shape. Let your spine be long and the back of your neck be soft.

CHILD'S POSE: Get on your knees and lower down so that your forehead goes towards the floor. If possible, extend your arms forward and rest here for a few breaths.

SIDE PLANK: Turn onto your side. Breathe and balance on one arm with your legs straight and stacked on top of one another. Then give it a try balancing with the other arm!

Which pose makes you happiest today?

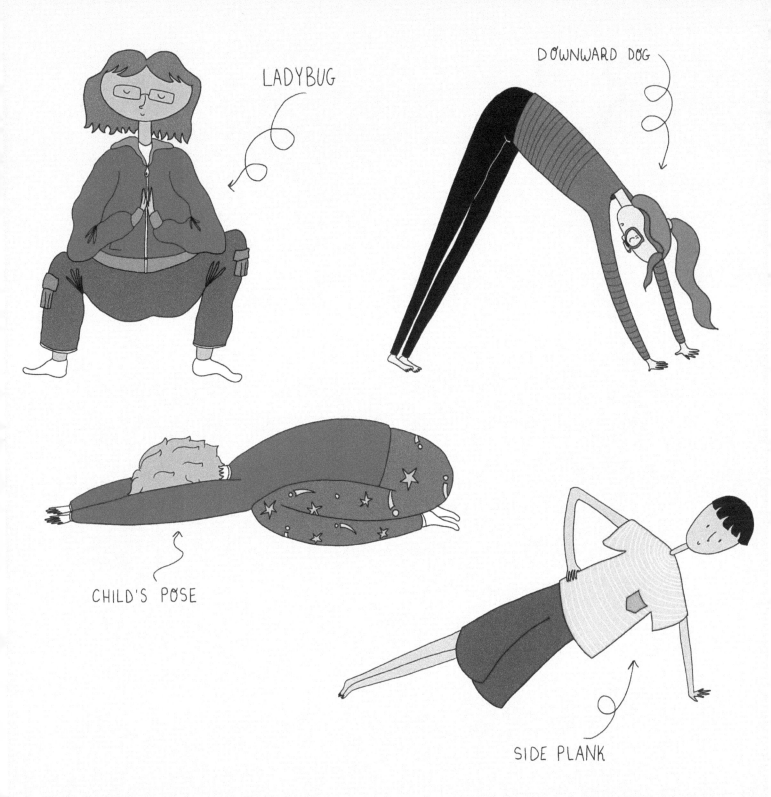

BUTTERFLY POSE: Sitting on the floor, bend your knees and put the bottoms of your feet together, like your favorite sandwich! You can stay still or lift and lower your knees like you are ready to fly.

If you could fly, where would you go?

TURTLE POSE: This pose is similar to butterfly pose, but try to lower your forehead toward your feet in any amount. Your back becomes like a turtle shell!

Do you ever like to hide in your shell like a turtle?

Can you guess which pose is which?

DANCER

BOAT

FORWARD FOLD

CHAIR

Try these poses and use a wall for support if you need it!

Come and sit like Ronnie with legs crossed and fingertips touching. Try sitting still without talking and see how your body feels after practicing some poses.

Do you have a favorite pose today?

Sitting still and being quiet like Ronnie can be tricky. Don't worry!

It may be helpful to close your eyes or lower your gaze in order to get focused. Listen.

What sounds or noises do you hear? The TV? Maybe someone talking? Your dog's collar is jingling? Someone sneezing? Honking of horns outside? Cows mooing?

People have been doing Yoga poses for years and years, practicing them over and over again, imitating shapes of animals, having fun, feeling good and getting calm.

Remember, Yoga is not about comparing or competing. It is about being in your beautiful body, making fun shapes with your body, and feeling good.

When we are peaceful and good to ourselves, we are good to others: people, pets, plants and our environment.

You can breathe and practice Yoga poses anywhere you go and can teach your friends and family, too!

Kids and adults practice Yoga around the world. Sometimes we practice Yoga alone or with (furry) friends and in groups.

Wherever we are, Yoga helps us to feel calm and peaceful. We can take good care of our bodies doing Yoga and take good care of each other when we are calm, centered, and feeling connected to our hearts.

Yoga helps us to be kind to ourselves, people in our family, and others in our community.

When we feel good and calm, we can send good thoughts to other people who may need some love and support. These people can be near or far away and can even be friends we have not met yet.

YAY FOR YOGA!

About the Author

President and CEO of Mari Fox Wellness, a lifestyle brand that helps kids, adults and seniors manage stress in healthy ways, Mari offers stress reduction classes and clean, self-care products that promote positive mental health and well-being.

Mari has had a passion for the arts and teaching since she was young, which inspired her to earn her Master of Education from The Ohio State University and K-12 Teaching Certification. She uses the magic of words, creativity, music and mindful movement to connect with children of all ages. In the ever-busy world, Mari invites children and adults of all ages to slow down, breathe and reminds us that Yoga and mindfulness are accessible and fun.

Mari lives with her life partner and doggy in Western New York.